This Book Belongs To

Name :

Phone :

Address :

Project Name : | Project No :

| Date :

Foreman : | Day :

Visitors

Schedule

Problems

Safety Issues

Summary Of Work

Signature :

Employee	Trade	Hours	Overtime

Equipment On Site	No. Units

Materials Delivered	No. Units	Equipment Rented	Rate

Others

Notes :

Project Name :

Project No :

Date :

Foreman :

Day :

Visitors	Schedule

Problems	Safety Issues

Summary Of Work

Signature :

Employee	Trade	Hours	Overtime

Equipment On Site	No. Units

Materials Delivered	No. Units	Equipment Rented	Rate

Others

Notes :

Project Name :

Foreman :

Project No :	
Date :	
Day :	

Visitors

Schedule

Problems

Safety Issues

Summary Of Work

Signature :

Employee	Trade	Hours	Overtime

Equipment On Site	No. Units

Materials Delivered	No. Units	Equipment Rented	Rate

Others

Notes :

Project Name :

Project No :

Date :

Foreman :

Day :

Visitors	Schedule

Problems	Safety Issues

Summary Of Work

Signature :

Employee	Trade	Hours	Overtime

Equipment On Site	No. Units

Materials Delivered	No. Units	Equipment Rented	Rate

Others

Notes :

Project Name : ________________________________

Foreman : ________________________________

| Project No : |
| Date : |
| Day : |

Visitors

Schedule

Problems

Safety Issues

Summary Of Work

Signature : ________________________________

Employee	Trade	Hours	Overtime

Equipment On Site	No. Units

Materials Delivered	No. Units	Equipment Rented	Rate

Others

Notes :

Project Name :

Foreman :

Project No :

Date :

Day :

Visitors	Schedule

Problems	Safety Issues

Summary Of Work

Signature :

Employee	Trade	Hours	Overtime

Equipment On Site	No. Units

Materials Delivered	No. Units	Equipment Rented	Rate

<table><tr><td align="center">Others</td></tr></table>

Notes :

Project Name : ____________________

Foreman : ____________________

Project No : ____________________

Date : ____________________

Day : ____________________

Visitors	Schedule

Problems	Safety Issues

Summary Of Work

Signature : ____________________

Employee	Trade	Hours	Overtime

Equipment On Site	No. Units

Materials Delivered	No. Units	Equipment Rented	Rate

<table><tr><td>Others</td></tr></table>

Notes :

Project Name :

Foreman :

Project No :

Date :

Day :

Visitors

Schedule

Problems

Safety Issues

Summary Of Work

Signature :

Employee	Trade	Hours	Overtime

Equipment On Site	No. Units

Materials Delivered	No. Units	Equipment Rented	Rate

<table>
<tr><th>Others</th></tr>
</table>

Notes :

Project Name :

Foreman :

Project No :

Date :

Day :

Visitors

Schedule

Problems

Safety Issues

Summary Of Work

Signature :

Employee	Trade	Hours	Overtime

Equipment On Site	No. Units

Materials Delivered	No. Units	Equipment Rented	Rate

Others

Notes :

Project Name :

Project No :

Date :

Foreman :

Day :

Visitors

Schedule

Problems

Safety Issues

Summary Of Work

Signature :

Employee	Trade	Hours	Overtime

Equipment On Site	No. Units

Materials Delivered	No. Units	Equipment Rented	Rate

Others

Notes :

Project Name : _______________________________

Foreman : _______________________________

Project No :	
Date :	
Day :	

Visitors

Schedule

Problems

Safety Issues

Summary Of Work

Signature : _______________________________

Employee	Trade	Hours	Overtime

Equipment On Site	No. Units

Materials Delivered	No. Units	Equipment Rented	Rate

Others

Notes :

Project Name :

Foreman :

Project No :

Date :

Day :

Visitors	Schedule

Problems	Safety Issues

Summary Of Work

Signature :

Employee	Trade	Hours	Overtime

Equipment On Site	No. Units

Materials Delivered	No. Units	Equipment Rented	Rate

Others

Project Name :

Project No :

Date :

Foreman :

Day :

Visitors	Schedule

Problems	Safety Issues

Summary Of Work

Signature :

Employee	Trade	Hours	Overtime

Equipment On Site	No. Units

Materials Delivered	No. Units	Equipment Rented	Rate

Others

Notes :

Project Name : _______________________________

____

Foreman : _______________________________

| Project No : |
| Date : |
| Day : |

Visitors

Schedule

Problems

Safety Issues

Summary Of Work

Signature : _______________________________ ✏

Employee	Trade	Hours	Overtime

Equipment On Site	No. Units

Materials Delivered	No. Units	Equipment Rented	Rate

Others

Notes :

Project Name :

Project No :

Date :

Foreman :

Day :

Visitors

Schedule

Problems

Safety Issues

Summary Of Work

Signature :

Employee	Trade	Hours	Overtime

Equipment On Site	No. Units

Materials Delivered	No. Units	Equipment Rented	Rate

Others

Notes :

Project Name :

Project No :

Date :

Foreman :

Day :

Visitors

Schedule

Problems

Safety Issues

Summary Of Work

Signature :

Employee	Trade	Hours	Overtime

Equipment On Site	No. Units

Materials Delivered	No. Units	Equipment Rented	Rate

Others

Notes :

Project Name :

Project No :

Date :

Foreman :

Day :

Visitors

Schedule

Problems

Safety Issues

Summary Of Work

Signature :

Employee	Trade	Hours	Overtime

Equipment On Site	No. Units

Materials Delivered	No. Units	Equipment Rented	Rate

Others

Notes :

Project Name :

Foreman :

Project No :

Date :

Day :

Visitors	Schedule

Problems	Safety Issues

Summary Of Work

Signature :

Employee	Trade	Hours	Overtime

Equipment On Site	No. Units

Materials Delivered	No. Units	Equipment Rented	Rate

<table>
<tr><th>Others</th></tr>
</table>

Notes :

Project Name :

Project No :

Date :

Foreman :

Day :

Visitors

Schedule

Problems

Safety Issues

Summary Of Work

Signature :

Employee	Trade	Hours	Overtime

Equipment On Site	No. Units

Materials Delivered	No. Units	Equipment Rented	Rate

Notes :

Project Name :

Project No :

Date :

Foreman :

Day :

Visitors	Schedule

Problems	Safety Issues

Summary Of Work

Signature :

Employee	Trade	Hours	Overtime

Equipment On Site	No. Units

Materials Delivered	No. Units	Equipment Rented	Rate

<table><tr><td>Others</td></tr></table>

Notes :

Project Name :

Foreman :

Project No :

Date :

Day :

Visitors	Schedule

Problems	Safety Issues

Summary Of Work

Signature :

Employee	Trade	Hours	Overtime

Equipment On Site	No. Units

Materials Delivered	No. Units	Equipment Rented	Rate

Others

Notes :

Project Name :

Project No :

Date :

Foreman :

Day :

Visitors	Schedule

Problems	Safety Issues

Summary Of Work

Signature :

Employee	Trade	Hours	Overtime

Equipment On Site	No. Units

Materials Delivered	No. Units	Equipment Rented	Rate

Others

Notes :

Project Name : ______________________________

Foreman : ______________________________

| Project No : |
| Date : |
| Day : |

Visitors

Schedule

Problems

Safety Issues

Summary Of Work

Signature : ______________________________

Employee	Trade	Hours	Overtime

Equipment On Site	No. Units

Materials Delivered	No. Units	Equipment Rented	Rate

Others

Notes :

Project Name :

Foreman :

Project No :

Date :

Day :

Visitors

Schedule

Problems

Safety Issues

Summary Of Work

Signature :

Employee	Trade	Hours	Overtime

Equipment On Site	No. Units

Materials Delivered	No. Units	Equipment Rented	Rate

Others

Notes :

Project Name : ____________________________

Foreman : ____________________________

Project No : ____________________________

Date : ____________________________

Day : ____________________________

Visitors

Schedule

Problems

Safety Issues

Summary Of Work

Signature : ____________________________

Employee	Trade	Hours	Overtime

Equipment On Site	No. Units

Materials Delivered	No. Units	Equipment Rented	Rate

Others

Notes :

Project Name : ______________________

Foreman : ______________________

Project No :

Date :

Day :

Visitors

Schedule

Problems

Safety Issues

Summary Of Work

Signature : ___________________

Employee	Trade	Hours	Overtime

Equipment On Site	No. Units

Materials Delivered	No. Units	Equipment Rented	Rate

Notes :

Project Name : ____________________

Foreman : ____________________

Project No : ____________________

Date : ____________________

Day : ____________________

Visitors

Schedule

Problems

Safety Issues

Summary Of Work

Signature : ____________________

Employee	Trade	Hours	Overtime

Equipment On Site	No. Units

Materials Delivered	No. Units	Equipment Rented	Rate

Others

Notes :

Project Name :

Project No :

Date :

Foreman :

Day :

Visitors	Schedule

Problems	Safety Issues

Summary Of Work

Signature :

Employee	Trade	Hours	Overtime

Equipment On Site	No. Units

Materials Delivered	No. Units	Equipment Rented	Rate

Others

Notes :

Project Name : | Project No :

| Date :

Foreman : | Day :

Visitors

Schedule

Problems

Safety Issues

Summary Of Work

Signature :

Employee	Trade	Hours	Overtime

Equipment On Site	No. Units

Materials Delivered	No. Units	Equipment Rented	Rate

Others

Notes :

Project Name :

Foreman :

Project No :

Date :

Day :

Visitors

Schedule

Problems

Safety Issues

Summary Of Work

Signature :

Employee	Trade	Hours	Overtime

Equipment On Site	No. Units

Materials Delivered	No. Units	Equipment Rented	Rate

www.ingramcontent.com/pod-product-compliance
Lightning Source LLC
LaVergne TN
LVHW041326200726
843509LV00009B/628